Coming to terms with disability

Coming to terms with disability

Selected writings

Bob Williams-Findlay

Resistance Books

Coming to terms with disability
Selected writings

Bob Williams-Findlay

Cover design: NJ Catchpole
Published July 2025
Resistance Books
info@resistancebooks.org
www.resistancebooks.org
ISBN: 978-1-872242-42-2 (pbk)
ISBN: 978-1-872242-43-9 (e-book)

Bob Williams-Findlay is the founder of Birmingham Disability Rights Group and the former Chair of the British Council of Organisations of Disabled People. He has written in various publications on the topic of disability politics, and is the author of *Disability Politics - the body as a site of struggle* (Pluto Press) and *More than a left foot* (Resistance Books).

CONTENTS

1. Disability politics and culture: Seeking a bridge over troubled waters   1

2. White lines and paradoxical relationships   45

3. Developing an eco-social approach towards self-determined living   73

4. My disability lexicon   93

1

Disability politics and culture: Seeking a bridge over troubled waters

Introduction

My book, *Disability Praxis*, was difficult to write and I had to compromise. With only 80,000 words to play with, many issues had to be left out or underdeveloped.[1] The past few months I have been exploring issues not fully covered in the book and I have run into difficulty for a variety of reasons.

From the beginning of my journey as a disabled scholar activist, I have found the minefield of language usage one of the main frustrations I have had to constantly deal with. The 21-year-old me, got into a debate about the name Union of the Physically Impaired Against Segregation (UPIAS).[2] I have never been comfortable with the words 'impairment' or 'handicapped'. Both I saw as extremely judgmental and demeaning. Today, I am happy to let golf and horse racing keep 'handicap'.

I did my utmost to disassociate it from disability, and I am partly responsible for the State and NHS replacing 'mental handicapped' with 'learning disability'; I advised the chair of working committee that reviewed services to learning disabled people.

For many years, I had doubts about talking in terms of 'disabled people' and I believe it remains problematic. In my two books, I talk about the dual identity that exists around the differing ways in which disability and therefore disabled people are made sense of.[3] It took me ages to grasp the idea that the social approach saw 'disabled people' as a collective identity around our positioning and situation within society; not as the description of the people themselves. So, what this means is that the term 'disabled people' has conflicting meanings associated with it.

I have reluctantly agreed to talk about impairment, even though I am sympathetic to some of the arguments against it. I dislike the fact that one of its meanings is 'flawed'. While I am accepting of the reality that the use of forceps resulted in me experiencing brain damage, I refuse to allow the judgmental evaluation of me as 'flawed'. I therefore compromise by viewing impairment as the altered state of an individual's body due to illness, disease, accident, or specific factors related to the individual's make up. Others, such as Deaf people and those from diverse Neurodiverse communities, would reject even this description.[4]

The cul-de-sacs we encounter and the troubled waters they create

As long ago as the 1920s people who had impairments questioned how they were being seen and spoken about. Members of 'The Disabled Society' argued they wanted to be regarded as 'disabled' rather than having one of the existing labels and identities imposed on them. Trying to make sense of who and what we are as people with bodies and minds that do not conform to set standards, has led us down many cul-de-sacs and in the process created troubled waters. One of the cul-de-sacs we have encountered is when trying to come up with descriptions which are counter normative definitions such as impairment and disability. I talk about being a person with Cerebral Palsy, not a spastic or a cerebral palsied person. Why? Because Cerebral Palsy doesn't define who I am. However, there are people who say they are Autistics and therefore don't subscribe to having an impairment. Likewise, I often am amused by Deaf people who say they are not disabled people, but claim disability benefits. Is this simply because they have no choice or is it more complex than that? I am not trying to deny a group's right to define who and what they are, but raise the fact that their decisions do not stand in isolation; they directly or indirectly impact upon others.

Recently someone tried to convince me that Elon Musk and Suella Braverman were disabled people under the social model. I pointed out that even back in Karl Marx's day, he dismissed this way of thinking as nonsense.[5] Yes, individuals in particular social relations may from time-to-time encounter impairment related discrimination, or be externally viewed as disabled as in this example, however the position they occupy within society means they are never part of a collective social group who are systematically subjected to social restrictions. Not all people with impairments are disabled people, but by having an impairment, they have the potential of becoming one if they encounter disablism on a regular basis and to the extent that it becomes socially restrictive.

Given what I have just stated, and the dual identity spoken of earlier, I would argue that the identities of 'disabled' person/people are surrounded by ambiguity. Let me attempt to explain what I mean by this.

Surrounded by ambiguity

Here are different ways in which people can be framed:

- A person may have a significant impairment, and as a consequence, could be viewed as being 'disabled' under the Equality Act. This does not necessarily mean the public/state/person accepts they are 'disabled'. The public/state could have a completely different take on the impairment compared to the individual as either side might evaluate the impairment reality in ways the other would not see or accept.

- A person may have a significant impairment; however, they might reject being viewed as disabled because they accept the dominant ways disability is defined and refuse to be associated with it.
- A person may have a significant impairment; however, they might reject being viewed as disabled in the traditional way because they *oppose* the dominant ways disability is defined and refuse to be associated with it.
- A person may or may not be seen to have a significant impairment because the reality associated with it might not be easily recognisable, therefore they might not be viewed as disabled because they don't 'fit' with the dominant ways disability is defined or understood by the public gaze.
- A person may have a significant impairment in terms of the public gaze; however, they might reject being viewed as impaired because they reject the dominant ways impairment/disability is defined and refuse to be associated with it.

- A person may have a significant impairment; however, they might be unaware of the social approach towards disability and therefore can't associate themselves with this way of seeing disability.

So we have people who see themselves as disabled directly through having an impairment; we have people who see themselves as disabled not directly as a consequence of having an impairment, but indirectly due to how society uses impairment reality against them by maintaining disabling barriers; then, finally there are those like Tom Shakespeare who see themselves as disabled by their impairments and society, or by their 'disabilities' (sic) and society.[6]

Does all this really matter?

Does all this really matter? Depends on how you view disability and disabled people's positioning within society – are they simply disadvantaged by their impairment/disability; discriminated against due to their impairment; or are they systematically oppressed by the nature of the social organisation of capitalist society? In passing, I would argue as a historical materialist, down the ages people with impairments have been both accepted and rejected according to a specific society's mode of production, belief systems, and social relations.[7] Such treatment however was largely in relation to individuals or particular impairment types. It was the arrival of capitalism that led to the creation of the systematic management of both impaired and unimpaired bodies.

The systematic management of significantly impaired bodies led to certain groups of people with impairments being subjected to 'unequal and differential treatment' which saw their exclusion from or marginalisation within mainstream social activities. This is identified as social oppression by disabled people's organisations. I subscribe to the view that there is a relationship between oppression and discrimination, but they are not one and the same. Nor is oppression experienced the same way between groups of those who are oppressed. The oppressive power relations stem from the needs of those that exercise that power – white nondisabled men generally speaking who own or work directly in the interest of Capital.

Approaching disablement, disability, as maintained by disablism

I see disability as a social situation – created by disablement and maintained by disablism – whereby people who do not conform to the contours of 'normality', which is socially constructed as 'ablebodiedness', are subjected to unequal and differential treatment as a consequence. Disability therefore is encountered to various degrees as marginalisation within or exclusion from mainstream social activities. Disability using the social approach is understood in terms of imposed social restriction, not an absence of bodily functional capacity. See *My Disability Lexicon* for definitions.[8]

Disablism maintains disabled people's oppression by controlling, through medicalisation, how their bodies and minds are evaluated in terms of social worth, in other words, use value. Some disabled people are, through various factors, assimilated because they manage to sell their labour. Those not accommodated face poverty, marginalised lifestyles, and warehousing/institutionalisation. How disabled people's 'bodies' are both seen and treated means the body has been a site of struggle.

Our bodies are controlled and devalued through medicalisation and social policy. We are denied bodily autonomy; thus prevented from meaningful self-management of our impairment reality. Elsewhere, I have acknowledged how the social approach/model became inward rather than outward looking.[9] I support Vic Finkelstein's view that this change in applying the social model is a mistake. I will continue, however, to also assert the view that there are differing, though connected, sites of struggle, but the radical social approach/model focuses on social change in the immediate circumstances through improving disabled people's lives, but with the ultimate objective of creating a transformative society to replace capitalist social relations.

The social model of disability a specific tool for a particular purpose

The social approach towards disability is based upon the UPIAS' interpretation of what disables people with physical impairments. Mike Oliver's social model of disability draws upon this and provides a way of focusing on disablement and disablism; that is, what is 'out there', the structures, systems, values, cultures, etc, that create and maintain the social restrictions/disabling barriers/disability, disabled people encounter. The model was not design to, nor is capable of, addressing personal experience of/encounters with the disablist society we come up against on a daily basis.[10]

What is required is other tools alongside the social model to engage in daily resistance taking place in specific sites of struggle. In *Disability Praxis,* I acknowledged the fact that disabled feminists raised important issues about personal experience of being disabled people, especially specific experiences of disabled women, and that important debates were marginalised or closed down.[11] There is an urgent need to revisit and in some instances resituate the issues that were raised within the dialogue around a new disability praxis which seeks the development of a social model of impairment and a new eco-social model of disability.

Everything said so far, is within my locker and I am comfortable with it, however, at the same time I am increasingly being troubled by what Finkelstein said almost 20 years ago concerning the undermining of the social approach towards disability; disability politics and culture. I see this happening through the importing of American cultural ideas as supplied by the likes of Andrew Pulrang, the eclectic thinking behind Fiona Campbell's 'ableism'; and of course, the neoliberal capitalist 'bio-psycho-social model', to name but a few key hostiles.[12] I am not in a position to address their ramifications here, but feel the need to acknowledge the fact that they inform the troubled waters I feel I am sinking deeper into.

Troubled waters surrounding disabled representation and disability culture

Since the end of 2023, I have been musing over disabled representation in film and TV, alongside the nagging debate about disability culture. I was prompted by the excitement over Dr Who's TARDIS getting a ramp.[13] Why do so many disabled people get ecstatic when a disabled character or 'disability related' issue appears on the big or little screen? I understand it in part in relation to our oppression and the invisibility we are subjected to, but is there more going on than this? Then there is an important question to be asked: what are we actually looking at? Recalling the earlier discussion on dual identity; is there a need to interrogate what constitutes a 'disabled character'? I believe such an interrogation is required because I am not convinced it is always possible to know how what is presented or viewed in terms of a 'disabled character' is being interpreted. This is due to the fact that what is offered and/or received could be from a multiple of perspectives.

A similar situation, I believe, arises within disability culture and disability art. In *My Disability Lexicon* I stand culture and art in opposition to disability. Hence disability art was an expression of a counter-culture. Increasingly, this radical interpretation is being replaced by a safer mainstream one: art done by disabled people/people with disabilities (sic). I see this as troubling, but exactly why, is and of itself, also troubling.

One definition of disability art is:

> Disability art or disability arts is any art, theatre, fine arts, film, writing, music or club that takes disability as its theme or whose context relates to disability.[14]

Do I/we agree with this definition? As argued within my MA dissertation, we cannot hold an assured view on this definition because an aspect of the context is missing. With more than one meaning and/or location for 'disability' existing, then talking about 'disability as a theme' is problematic because it is shrouded by ambiguity. From my perspective, I have argued:

> Disability art is the production of material that recounts or challenges disabled people's lived experience of unequal and differential treatment.
>
> However, this was placed within the context of seeing it as part of the cultures developed by disabled people in their struggle for emancipation from disability. It is therefore a political counter-culture which rejects 'normality' and societal evaluation of living lives with impairments.
>
> As an aside, I view the idea of rejecting 'normality' and societal evaluation of living lives with impairments' as enabling disabled people, collectively and individually, to appraise and articulate how they wish their impairment reality

to be acknowledged and addressed. This would allow space for the direction of travel found within the Affirmation model of disability, and Paul Abbley's way of addressing impairment from a position of ambivalence where it is possible to have mixed feelings or contradictory ideas about the existence of impairment.[15]

As I have stated, within my perspective, disability arts are about portraying living within and combatting a disablist society in order to express one's community and self. In other words, to reveal what has been hidden and to transcend the oppressive stereotyping of disabled people and their lifestyles. This, I would argue, is a different art form to that which sees people who are considered disabled, doing art. Another definition I have come across is this one:

> Disability art is different from Disability in the arts which refers more to the active participation or representation of disabled people in the arts rather than the context of the work being about disability.[16]

Personally, from my perspective, I can accept this distinction because it can be viewed as 'practice which promotes social inclusion', and as such, through participation challenges both disability and disablism.

The problem comes, of course, when it is not presented in this way.

So far, I have spoken of disability art in terms of production by disabled people, however, I have to acknowledge there is also the view that says: 'Disability art does not require the maker of the art to be disabled.'[17] In one sense there is a political logic and understanding to this because people who are not members of an oppressed group can be allies by relaying experience of a particular oppression – I have, for example, written a play highlighting misogyny and women's assumed role as 'care givers' – however, as an ally, I took my lead from women's own stories. So, nondisabled people can and should engage in disability art production, but only if there are forms of coproduction involved. If not, I would regard it to be both disempowering and a form of cultural misappropriation.

I want to return to the point I made earlier about being troubled by how disability art as an expression of a radical counter-culture was increasingly being replaced by a safer mainstream one which sees disability art as any form of art that happens to be done by disabled people. Clearly, I do not want to see the embryonic forms of a radical counter-culture lost or simply watered down and assimilated into the mainstream where 'disability' is viewed purely as a personal characteristic, however, I also said I was troubled by having thoughts along these lines.

Why I am troubled by how 'disabled identities' are addressed, is that the relationships between impairment reality, and collective and individual identities have become hostages to fortune. One of the ways I have been trying to navigate out of these troubled waters is to put forward the view that disabled people engage in paradoxical relationships which do not simply come about due to the unequal and differential treatment created by disablement and disablism; but they also involve mediating living with impairment reality through interaction between ourselves and encountered social environments which includes interpersonal relationships. To fully grasp the paradoxical nature of these relationships requires us to acknowledge that disablement provides some context.

The fact that people with impairments exist within a society designed, built, managed and consumed by the majority of human beings who are unlike them, means this has always had consequences for those of us who are subjected to disablism. We discussed this previously, but it is useful to remind ourselves that UPIAS defined '... disability as the disadvantage or restriction of activity caused by a contemporary social organisation *which takes no or little account of people who have physical impairments* and thus excludes them from participation in the mainstream of social activities.' (Emphasis added – BWF)[18]

While I believe the outcome of the impact of 'a contemporary social organisation' i.e., capitalist society, is captured here, what is absent is the ideological aspect of the creation of disablement. I would argue what is missing is the dialectic of disability; because it is *precisely how people with impairments are 'taken into account'*, in the sense of being subjected to negative evaluations and as consequence devalued, that ultimately leads to society taking little or no account of them. Without this dialectical understanding, the cause of social oppression can be simply viewed as stemming from 'ignorance' or 'forgetfulness'.

I wish to forward the view that the dialectic of disability – the tensions and contradictions found within people with impairments desire to be included in a society that, by its very nature and design, has discarded and disregarded them – has led to the existence of paradoxical relationships. Disabled people can find themselves in contradictory situations whereby they can be both accepted and rejected, included and excluded, have dual identities, be valued and devalued, etc, depending on what is taking place at any specific time or circumstances. Thus is the nature of disabled people's social situation.

Being of this world, but not truly part of it

The dialectics of disability are central to the nature of disabled people's social situation, whereby they are of this world, but not truly part of it. In a generalised sense, the way society sees disability and disabled people has produced not only paradoxical relationships but also a paradoxical gaze between people with and without impairments which pictures each as 'alien' to the other. In the eyes of the majority of people, those with significant impairments are viewed as, and at the same time, treated as 'Other'. Jenny Morris in *Pride Against Prejudice* discusses assumptions regarding disabled people, both in terms of absences within culture, but also the distortions:

> Surely, the representation and exploration of human experience is incomplete as long as disability is either missing from or misrepresented in all the forms that cultural representation takes. It is fear and denial of the frailty, vulnerability, mortality and arbitrariness of human experience that deters us from confronting such realities. Fear and denial prompt the isolation of those who are disabled, ill or old as 'other,' as 'not like us.[19]

So, for many disabled people they have been made to feel 'of this world, but not truly part of it'. The above quotation from Morris also highlights the ambiguity around definitions and identifying as 'disabled'. As I said earlier, disability politics focus on changing social relations within society, but this has come at a high price in my opinion.

By focusing on changing what's going on 'out there', I believe the Disabled People's Movement neglected addressing at the same time the nature and impact of dominant ideologies on how disabled people often either internalise their oppression or lose their own sense of self. So while disabled feminists were right to raise issues around living with impairments in a disablist society, these issues are about personal experiences and encounters with disablism, not the collective structural social restrictions that the social model was designed to explore. Clearly, there is a relationship between them, but nonetheless they relate to differing sites of struggle. Too little has been done to explore the impact our oppressive imposed identity has had on ourselves, individually, and on other disabled people, collectively.

Like most other oppressed sections of society, disabled people have had very few visible role models to rely on. Even today, the presentation of disabled people in the mass media or sport, remains framed either by the imposed identity or through a commodified cultural individualistic reversal of the dominant ways disabled people are viewed. Instead of the traditional 'Othering', disabled people – often spoken of as 'people with disabilities' (sic) – are encouraged to 'big up' their identity around the diversity contained within their own embodiment.

On a personal level, growing up 'invisible', without role models 'out there', meant I was never encouraged to be 'me' as I was not allowed to question who or what I was. The expectation was to be come as 'normal' as possible which, I would argue, distorted and held back any sense of self. While fully rejecting the ideological assertion that the nature and degree of a person's impairment is the direct cause of their social disadvantage, it is nonetheless a fact that our impairment reality is used against us. This point relates to Abberley's assertion about disabled people's inferiority; it is the nature of our impairment reality that leads to society singling us out for differential treatment. It is still the case that our 'self' is dressed in negativity with the expectation that we compare ourselves to others we have either never been like or are representative of our former selves.

Often people's first encounter with 'takes on impairment' is through the medical or public social gaze. Rarely, although it happens, is our first encounter with alternative takes on impairment via engagement with people who have first-hand acknowledge and experience of what we are going through. What this means is more often than not, our lives as people with impairments begin with a distorted view of reality. To add insult to injury, once 'impairment' is acknowledged or denied through medical or public social gazes, then they are likely to encounter various forms of disablism.

The failure of materialist disabled scholar activists to adequately explore the 'individual tragedy model' beyond how it underpins disabled people's experience of discrimination, opened the door to postmodernist critiques which reject to various degrees the foundations of the materialist grounding of the social interpretation of disability. As a result, most postmodernist critiques focus on the cultural aspects of the dominant gaze.

What has all this to do with the issues that are troubling me? I want to try and address this question through a slight recap which begins with a quotation from Vic Finkelstein where he asserts:

> There is, of course, a profound difference between struggles based upon an analysis concerned with the processes leading to the creation of disability (the social construction of disability as a socio-economic relationship) and struggles based on reflections of the experience of disablement (or our conscious reflections on living with an impairment in a disabling world and interpreting the state of disability as a psycho-social experience).[20]

I agree with the distinction he makes between these two kinds of struggles. The first set are about dealing with the social situation and changing the socio-economic relationship; requiring a collective response. This draws upon the social approach towards disability and focuses on the *nature of society*. The second set of struggles are not about dealing with the social situation through a transformative change agenda. Instead, they are concerned with either coming to terms with, or seeking to address the consequences of living with an impairment in and of itself within disablist social environments. Attempting to address these two sets of struggles as if they one and the same and doing so through employing the social model was, and continues to be, a disastrous path to travel.

The social model approach is concerned with the material world 'out there'; the social organisation of society. The main thrust of disability politics, as previously noted, has been to emancipate disabled people – end institutionalisation and to create inclusive communities – by removing the obstacles that stand in their way. Oliver outlined the approach underlying the social model when he wrote:

> Using the generic term [disabled people] does not mean that I do not recognise differences in experience within the group but that in exploring this we should start from the ways oppression

differentially impacts on different groups of people rather than with differences in experience among individuals with different impairments.[21]

While I broadly agree with this approach, the difficulty lies in how 'we should start from the ways oppression differentially impacts on different groups of people' has been or should be interpreted. I believe this leads us back to asking questions about how disabled people encounter oppression and how they view themselves. Finkelstein, as we saw earlier, spoke about 'the state of disability as a psycho-social experience', and I want to argue that I believe this is what many refer to as internalised oppression.

This invites us to review what is meant by oppression. Earlier, I suggested a distinction needs to be made between oppression and discrimination because I subscribe to the way John Chalton defines oppression as:

> ... a phenomenon of power in which relations between people and between groups are experienced in terms of domination and subordination, superiority and control. Those with power control; those without power lack control. Power presupposes political, economic and social hierarchies, structured relations of groups of people, and a system or regime of power.

This system, the existing power structure, encompasses the thousands of ways some groups and individuals impose control over others.[22]

The power over disabled people, I would argue, is not simply exercised through direct or indirect forms of discriminatory practices, but is conducted through a myriad of different forms of control. What is often neglected in our analysis of disablement, disability, and disablism is the ways in which being subjected to unequal and differential treatment does not only impact upon disabled people at a macro level of society, but also at a micro level. The social model has mainly been used to explore and address the disabling nature of policies, procedures, practices, alongside challenging oppressive attitudes and cultures that exclude and vilify disabled people. It has been used to create 'reforms' and improve lives within the system. However, as a result of looking at 'the ways oppression differentially impacts on different groups of people rather than with differences in experience among individuals with different impairments' there has been a lack of attention paid to the consequences of living with impairments in a disablist material world.

There is a debate to be had in terms of how internalised oppression and 'false consciousness' are discussed in relation to each other. False consciousness is often described as 'the idea that those from subordinate sectors of society systematically hold beliefs that are caused by the distortions of those in power in society and that these beliefs ultimately keep the subordinate in their subordinate conditions.'

Hernandez-Saca and Cannon inform us that:

> From a Marxist historical materialist perspective, Charlton (1998) writes about the consciousness of disabled people as they experience internalized oppression through their alienation by the hegemonic and dominant worldview of the status quo that 'naturalizes superiority and inferiority, power and powerlessness' that he argues characterizes 'the internalization of oppression that creates an emasculation of the self' (p. 69). Charlton (1998) continues by defining this latter social process as disabled people incorporating a false consciousness due to the internalized oppression that results in a sense of powerlessness.[23]

Within, *Nothing About Us, Without Us,* Charlton put forward the view that the absorption of the hegemonic and dominant worldview, which locates disability within an individual's body and the cause of their inferiority, leads to false consciousness arising from internalised oppression.

He goes on to say:

The replacement of the false consciousness of self-pity and helplessness with the raised consciousness of dignity, anger, and empowerment has meaningfully affected the way in which many people with disabilities relate personally and politically to society.[24]

It is not my intention to throw the baby out with the bathwater, but I am not wholly satisfied with this approach. In my book, *Disability Praxis,* I wanted to air a note of caution by saying:

The [Disabled People's] Movement attracted people who, to various degrees, had become aware of disability as a political or social issue through self-awareness or having contact with its ideas. Shakespeare is right to say people are socialised into how they view disability; however, he underplays the pervasive nature of societal approaches towards disability. Due to the exclusionary practices of disablism, it has always been difficult for people with impairments to 'discover' alternatives to seeing disability as other than 'a personal tragedy'. Making parallels with the Marxist concept of 'false consciousness' and the feminist approach towards 'internalised oppression' in the manner he suggests is unhelpful. This said, I do believe there is a debate to be had in relation to 'internalised oppression', but not necessarily in terms of political consciousness raising *in the first instance.* [BWF emphasis added][25]

I sought to address how I viewed internalised oppression by saying:

Paulo Freire, when working with the oppressed poor in Latin America, noted that a characteristic of those who are oppressed is self-depreciation. Micheline Mason explains this observation well: It would not exist without the real external oppression that forms the social climate in which we exist ... Once oppression has been internalised, little force is needed to keep us submissive. We harbour inside ourselves the pain and the memories, the fears and the confusions, the negative self-images and the low expectations, turning them into weapons with which to re-injure ourselves.[26]

Without going into too much detail, I believe rather than talk about 'false consciousness', it is more useful to speak in terms of what Antonio Gramsci called, 'hegemony'. To summarise what this is and how it operates, I am employing certain quotations from Raymond Williams.[25]

Williams's key points include the following:

1. *Hegemony constitutes lived experience,* 'a sense of reality for most people in the society, a sense of absolute because experienced reality beyond which it is very difficult for most members of the society to move, in most areas of their lives.' (p.100). I view this to be an explanation as to why dominant ideologies around disability are so difficult to throw off. Disability as a 'negative personal problem' is entrenched within 'common sense' and existing social relations. This 'common sense' aligns with societal normative values and produce a lethal cocktail which means disabled people become invisibilised not only within how they are both seen and treated, but also because of the absences the cocktail creates in people's consciousness.

2. *Hegemony exceeds ideology* 'in its refusal to equate consciousness with the articulate formal system which can be and ordinarily abstracted as "ideology".' (p.109). What I understand by this statement is that hegemony includes the power to establish "legitimate" definitions of social needs and authoritative definitions of social situations.'

3. *Lived hegemony is a process, not a system or structure* (though it can be schematized as such for the purposes of analysis). How disabled people encounter disablism is an example of this.
4. *Hegemony is dynamic,* 'It does not just passively exist as a form of dominance. It has continually to be renewed, recreated, defended, and modified. It is also continually resisted, limited, altered, challenged by pressures not all its own'. In the latter parts of *Disability Praxis,* I believe I give concrete examples of how this has been a core element within the struggle for emancipation and the push back from the agents and institutions of Capital.
5. *Hegemony attempts to neutralize opposition***,** 'the decisive hegemonic function is to control or transform or even incorporate [alternatives and opposition].' (p.113). Again, this is evident in how the World Health Organisation responded to disability politics via its International Classification of Functioning and the incorporation of Independent Living in the United Nation's Convention on the Rights of Disabled People.
6. *Hegemony* is not necessarily total, 'It is misleading, as a general method, to reduce all political and cultural initiatives and

contributions to the terms of the hegemony.' 'Authentic breaks within and beyond it ... have often in fact occurred.'

Taken all together, I see disablism and its hegemonic power as being more than the oppressive ideas from dominant ideologies, the discriminatory practices it fosters; it also exists in the daily negation of the very existence of disabled people. Our invisibility and the creation of stereotypes seriously damages how we see ourselves both individually and collectively. This, in my opinion, is the essence of the internalised oppression disabled people experience especially through being seen and treated as 'Other' as spoken about earlier. UPIAS, however, expressed concern over the notion of internalised oppression because of the risk that discussions could return to the focusing on individualised experiences rather than the social causes of oppression. However, many escapees from institutional living believe they must both learn and unlearn how to relate to themselves as disabled people when transferring from a segregated impairment-focused environment into a primarily non-disabled culture, which at the time was alien to them.[28]

At a micro level of society: within communities, workplaces, leisure, services, families – i.e., their interactions in the material world – disabled individuals are not only dealing with hostile and disabling social environments, but that the oppressive treatment also can, and often does, cause emotional and psychological harm. I believe the activists working within the materialist approach have surrendered ground to those who employ the idealist one in relation to this site of struggle.

This surrendering of ground has had many roots. I see the growth of 'identity politics' as one source, but this also links with the demise of the Disabled People Movement. How then does the concept of internalised oppression relate to the disability politics of the present? Internalised oppression is often described as:

> Internalized oppression occurs as a result of psychological injury caused by external oppressive events (e.g., harassment and discrimination), and it has a negative impact on individuals' self-system (e.g., self-esteem, self-image, self-concept, self-worth, and self-regulation). The trauma of internalized oppression is amplified by repetitive exposure to explicit violence such as segregation and discrimination, as well as implicitly through various forms of oppressive microprocesses and insidious microaggressions (e.g., privation of inclusion and peripheralizing – [what I call exclusion and marginalisation – BWF]). It may manifest on an individual or group level, and may

form as base for in-group conflict and further discrimination that can be hurtful and limiting.[29]

What is troubling for me is knowing that Finkelstein was a professional NHS psychologist, yet he dismissed the idea of internalised oppression as part of his approach towards the psychology of disability. Did he view the idea of internalised oppression as being an 'outside in' approach? Can this troubling fact be made sense of? My starting point is the remind ourselves that within dominant ideologies around 'disability', it is the person's lack of measured functional capacity which lays the foundations for their social disadvantages. The focus of 'a cure' – both medical and social – is inward facing; fixing the person. UPIAS' social interpretation of disability by breaking the direct causal link between the impairment (impairment reality which is negatively measured as 'disability'), and social disadvantage (the social restrictions imposed on top of impairment reality due to how it is reacted to within the social organisation of society), altered the focus of attention. The new focus was purely on seeking 'a cure' for the ills of capitalism through social change 'out there' and not personal change.

Given this shift away from the 'inward' – fixing the person – towards an 'outward' focus – fixing society; I believe Finkelstein was concerned about dragging 'disability' back into being 'a personal problem' if the emotional and psychological harm done to individuals by disablism is seen as internalised oppression.

A number of important issues flow from my reading of the situation. Firstly, emotional and psychological harm are considered to be things linked to mental ill-health and therefore part of the realm of medical professionals such as psychologists. While not ignoring or dismissing this link, I believe the description outlined earlier gives an alternative way to viewing internalised oppression. Secondly, as I suggested earlier, another consideration we need to make is that in the work of both Finkelstein and Oliver, as Abberley points out, the relationship between oppression and discrimination is far from clear and they are often collapsed together. Finally, it is unfortunate, but it is evident in their work that disabled feminists such as Morris, French, Crow and Thomas, do misrepresent the purpose of the social model and the idea of 'the personal as political'.[30] I explain why I hold this opinion in my book and also why I find fault with how disabled male scholar activists reacted to the questions being posed.

While I see the social model as having no direct role in addressing the personal experiences of encountering disabling situations; I contend that the social approach does feature, however, this is in relation to specific contexts. Unlike Finkelstein, I believe we should not dismiss altogether the existence of internalised oppression. A crucial aspect of this acknowledgement has to be the differences that exist between oppression and discrimination, the interaction between them, and the insights this provides for not only our understanding of the need to develop disability culture, but also in terms of how people with impairments have to confront who and what they are.

I see no contradiction in seeing disabled people's oppression as stemming from a particular socio-economic relationship, while at the same time acknowledging the war of attrition disabled people engage in both consciously and subconsciously. Disabled people's identities, lifestyles, social worth, etc, are as I suggested earlier, all caught within the dialectics of disability.

The last thirty years has witnessed a socio-political global shift to the right, where the policies of neoliberalism have undermined the welfare state, increased commodification, encouraged self-reliance and individualism. Face with this, the disabled people's movement went into decline, the radical social model, disability politics, and culture, was watered down. The idealist approach, as Finkelstein noted in 2001, 'is perfectly at home with the "rights" approach that is increasingly dominating the British disability movement and characterises the USA movement.'[31] The idealist approach in some people's hands leads to this absurd conclusion: 'Disabled people need a stronger social model that acts as a means to a society which enables and ensures their rights; the right to live a dignified life, as well as to live in an environment that enables people to flourish with disability.' [32] The dialectics of disability are completely ignored, that is recognising disabled people are struggling to be accepted in a society that rejects them.

Disability politics and culture in the current climate

UPIAS was quite clear in its belief that what united disabled people was not the actual existence of impairments, but rather the oppressive social relations people experienced as a result of having impairments. Finkelstein suggested that an understanding of the psychology of disability must start from the principle that 'we make sense of our world according to the way we experience it': 'If disabled people are denied access to mainstreamed social activities, we will not only have different experiences to that of our able-bodied peers but we will interpret the world differently; we will see it, think about it, have feelings about it and talk about it differently. The question is, however, "from what standpoint should this psychological experience be interpreted?"'

Finkelstein argued:

... [that as most things are] 'made sense of 'through the lived experiences of non-disabled people, this means the development of an understanding of the psychology of disability has been prevented. Disabled people's own interpretations of the world have been ignored, not allowed to develop or simply denied because they are regarded as subjective and therefore not valid.[33]

This is why I link the concept of internalised oppression with the dialectics of disability and the paradoxical relationships that exist for disabled people as a result. It is also why I believe disability culture is important; although the failure to address the impact of how and why disabled people have had their impairments used against them has led to the idealist distortions within the promoting of disability politics and culture. The radical social approach towards disability was right to break the causal link between impairment and disability, but in so doing, neglected the significance of the fact that as most things are 'made sense of' through the lived experiences of non-disabled people, including the absence of living with significant impairments. The underplaying of linking the concept of internalised oppression with the dialectics of disability means disability politics in the hands of the idealists has resulted in the rejection of the breaking the causal link between impairment and disability, situating and presenting impairment reality in terms of 'embodiment', and replacing the materialist understanding of disablism with accounts of 'ableism'.

This shift in disability politics over the last thirty years has created troubled waters. The shifts, as noted, relate to shifts in mainstream politics as well.

As one disabled activist put it to me:

> The barriers to true independent living, and how we experience the world, undoubtedly inform our experiences! Yet oppression is our real lived experience [of] the threat of institutional care, how we are educated and approaches towards our health. [This treatment] realises the oppression of our autonomy, our voice and diverse range of experiences.

Here lies the essence of the troubled waters. The denial of disabled people's autonomy, their collective voice and promotion of their diverse range of experiences has led to their lives and 'selves' being externally defined and controlled. The last thirty years has seen the reversing of the positive gains made by disabled people. Neoliberal social and economic policies have ensured that the impaired body has become a site of struggle in part through commodification relating to 'Social Care' (sic) and employment, on the one hand, and the promotion of self-reliance and eugenic based values, on the other.

Just as the false dream of 'full civil and human rights' was being embraced, the harsh realities of the age of austerity came along to turn the dream into a nightmare. The imported American cultural and idealist views fused with the rights agenda and the bio-psycho-social model as represented by the World Health Organisation's International Classification of Functioning (ICF), and United Nations' Convention on the Rights of Persons with Disabilities (sic) Against this backdrop, the radical ideas which informed both disability politics and culture were abandoned, thus the only visible way 'to make sense of the world' was to work with and against the lived experiences of non-disabled people.[34] As a consequence, the 'identity politics' coming from the USA operate from an idealist and individualised basis. Thus, 'disability pride' becomes the articulation of what I call a 'reverse mirror' which sets out to turn 'bad', 'negative', 'unacceptable', ways of viewing and treating people and their 'disabilities' (sic) into 'good', 'positive' and 'acceptable' ones.

Does this 'celebrate disability' approach address the real issues around impairment production, capitalist social relations, and the need for a transformative society? I would argue that the real issues become hidden within the 'reverse mirror' which sees reflected the rejection of 'blaming the disabled' (sic) and switching things so that the blame falls on the bogey 'able' instead. Here is where I require a tin hat because I want to forward the view that this is a by-product of internalised oppression.

Having stated my position, I return to why I am troubled. The lack of attention paid to impairment reality, especially in relation to living in a disablist society, means that disability politics only promoted a partial understanding of disability culture – the lived experience of 'making sense of', living within and seeking to resist, a disabling society. Art production is part of this, and as I said earlier, I see disability art as resistance and representation of disabled people in opposition to disability. It is a tool to assist disabled people 'to make sense of' the world through their experience which includes facing oppression, but also impairment reality because the body is a site of struggle.

The issue here, and my trouble within troubled waters, is that everything I have written about makes the present 'world of disability art' problematic. The dual identity, the conflation of impairment reality and disability again, the depoliticisation of disabled communities, the 'celebrate disability' cultural promotion, all contribute to the uncertainty as to what disability art is in today's world. Much of this troubling I have related to the question of social and political consciousness.

When a person with cerebral palsy, for example, paints a vase of flowers; is this no different to someone without an impairment undertaking the painting? I am not focusing so much on the functioning side of things, but rather what the artist brings to the canvas. Recalling paradoxical relationships and the psychology of disability, maybe there is more to the sites of struggle disabled people battle on than meets the 'eye'...

Notes

1. Williams-Findlay B., Disability Praxis, London: Pluto Press, 2023.
2. Priestley M., Finkelstein V. & Davis K., 'Fundamental Principles of Disability', Union of the Physically Impaired Against Segregation, 1975.
3. Williams-Findlay B., *More Than a Left Foot*, London: Resistance Books, 2020.
4. Chapman R., Empire of Normality Neurodiversity and Capitalism, London: Pluto Press, 2023.
5. 'As an individual I am "lame", but money provides me with twenty-four leges. Therefore, I am not lame'. Marx K., *Early writings 1818-1883*, Harmondsworth; New York: Penguin Books in association with New Left Review, 1992.
6. Shakespeare T., *Disability Rights and Wrongs*, London: Routledge, 2006
7. Russell M. & Malhotra R., 'Capitalism and Disability', *Socialist Register*, Vol. 38, 2002.
8. Williams-Findlay B., 'My Disability Lexicon', 2022, https://mtalf.home.blog/2022/09/06/my-disability-lexicon/.
9. Finkelstein V., 'Outside, "Inside Out"', *Coalition,* GMCDP, 1996, pp.30-36.
10. Oliver M., Understanding Disability: From Theory to Practice, London: Macmillan Press,1996.
11. *Disability Praxis* – See Chapter 7.
12. Pulrang D., '3 Ways Disability Culture Has Been Changing', Forbes, 2021, https://www.forbes.com/sites/andrewpulrang/2021/09/23/3-ways-disability-culture-has-been-changing/; Campbell F. K., 'Ableism: A Theory of Everything? Ableism, Racism and Conflicts of Participation & Inclusion in Society and

the Labour Market', Hamburg, Germany, 2014, https://youtu.be/dY3EMNaB5p0; Barile M., 'Globalization and ICF Eugenics: Historical Coincidence or Connection? The More Things Change the More They Stay the Same', *Disability Studies Quarterly*, Spring, Vol. 23, No. 2, 2003, pp. 208–23.

13. Griffen L., 'Doctor Who's Tardis "getting a wheelchair ramp to accommodate upcoming characters"', *Metro*, 2022, https://metro.co.uk/2022/06/30/doctor-whos-tardis-getting-wheelchair-ramp-to-accommodate-upcoming-characters-16921999/.
14. *'Disability Arts. A Brief History'*, Shape, Archived from the original on 22 February 2012, http://www.shapearts.org.uk/abriefhistory.aspx.
15. Swain J., & French S., 'Towards an Affirmation Model of Disability', *Disability & Society*, 15(4), 2000, pp.569–582; 'Disability in the arts', Wikipedia, https://en.wikipedia.org/wiki/Disability_in_the_arts#:~:text=Disability%20in%20the%20arts%20is%20an%20aspect%20within,work%20of%20specific%20painters%20and%20those%20who%20draw.
Abberley P., 'The Concept of Oppression and the Development of A Social Theory of Disability', in *Disability Studies: Past Present and Future*, Len Barton and Mike Oliver (eds.), Leeds: The Disability Press, 1997, pp.160–78.
16. Disability art https://alchetron.com/Disability-art
17. Ibid.
18. Finkelstein V., 'Phase 2: Discovering the Person in "Disability" and "Rehabilitation"', *Magic Carpet*, Vol XXVII (1), 1975, pp.31-38; Williams-Findlay B., *Disability Praxis*, pp.97.

19. Morris J., *Pride Against Prejudice*, London: Women's Press, 1991, pp.,85.
20. Finkelstein V., 'Outside, "Inside Out"', pp.33.
21. Mike O., 'Capitalism, Disability and Ideology: A Materialist Critique of the Normalization', Leeds: University of Leeds, 1994, https://disability-studies.leeds.ac.uk/wp-content/uploads/sites/40/library/Oliver-cap-dis-ideol.pdf, pp.3.
22. Charlton J. I., Nothing About Us Without Us: Disability Oppression and Empowerment, California: University of California Press,1998.
23. Hernandez-Saca D. I. & Cannon M., 'Disability as Psycho-Emotional Disablism: A Theoretical and Philosophical Review of Education Theory and Practice', in Peters, M. (ed.), *Encyclopaedia of Educational Philosophy and Theory*. Springer, Singapore, 2016.
24. J. Charlton, *Nothing About Us Without Us*, 1st Edition, University of California Press, 1998.
25. Williams-Findlay B., *Disability Praxis*, pp.45.
26. Williams-Findlay B., *Disability Praxis*, pp.77-8.
27. Williams J., *Keywords: A Vocabulary of Culture and Society*, Revised Edition. New York: Oxford University Press,1985.
28. Williams-Findlay, *More Than a Left Foot,* London: Resistance Books, 2020, Chapter Six 'When B. Two Worlds Collide'.
29. Case A. D. & Hunter C. D., 'Counterspaces: a unit of analysis for understanding the role of settings in marginalized individuals' adaptive responses to oppression', *American Journal of Community Psychology*. 50 (1-2), 2012, pp.257-270.
30. See for example: Thomas C., *Female Forms: Experiencing and Understanding Disability,* Buckingham: Open

University Press, 1999; Morris J., 'Feminism and Disability', *Feminist Review,* Vol. 43, Spring, 1993, pp.57-70, 68; French S., 'Disability, Impairment or Something in Between?', in *Disabling Barriers - Enabling Environments*, Swain J., French S., Barnes C. & Thomas C., eds., London: Sage, 1993.

31. Finkelstein V., 'The Social Model of Disability Repossessed', Manchester Coalition of Disabled People, 2001.
32. Berghs, M., Atkin, K., Hatton, C., & Thomas, C., 'Do disabled people need a stronger social model: a social model of human rights?', *Disability & Society*, 34 (7-8), 2019, pp.1034-39.
33. Williams-Findlay B., *Disability Praxis*, pp.176; Finkelstein V., 'Experience and Consciousness' (Notes for 'Psychology of Disability' Talk), Liverpool Housing Authority, 1990.
34. World Health Organisation, International Classification of Functioning, Disability and Health (ICF) (Geneva: WHO, 2001), www.who.int/ classifications/icf/en/. United Nations Convention on the Rights of Disabled People (UN acknowledge language self-determination), https://humanrights.gov.au/our-work/disability-rights/united-nations-convention-rights-persons-disabilities-uncrpd.

COMING TO TERMS WITH DISABILITY

2

White lines and paradoxical relationships

Preamble

This piece comes from a request that I write about my experiences and feelings as a disabled supporter attending or watching sporting activities undertaken by mainly nondisabled participants. Having given this request considerable thought, I have decided to address the issues involved from a number of positions because the identity of being a 'disabled supporter' is not the only identity that I have. Rather than simply focus on the sport / supporter paradoxical relationship, I have elected to place this in a wider context and situate it within the overall framing of living with a significant impairment in a disablist society.

It is not my aim to over complicate things, however, I believe my personal experiences and feelings cannot be understood without exploring why and how I am a disabled person and, at the same time, acknowledge that I am also part of collective encountered oppression. For fifty years I have been politically conscious of the fact I belong to a social group whose members are subjected to 'unequal and differential treatment'; however this consciousness does not exist evenly within the group. Some disabled people passively accept the officially sanctioned reasoning behind being labelled as 'disabled'; others reject the label and any association with 'them'. Those with a political consciousness hold a spectrum of positions in relation to their situation.

When I undertook disability equality training, I was mindful not to offer anecdotes because it was important to ensure the ideas being conveyed could not be dismissed as 'the exception to the rule' or become over individualised around my own life's journey. In this piece I am going to talk personally about my experiences, but I believe many disabled people could offer similar accounts. The paradoxical relationships discussed will be situated within the context of interactions that see me in the roles of participator and spectator.

Introduction

The paradoxical relationships disabled people have are not just about the unequal and differential treatment created by disablement and disablism; it also involves mediating living with impairment reality through interaction between ourselves and encountered social environments. From a personal perspective, I will be discussing these issues frequently moving between the personal and political; considering tensions and contradictions through the application of theory and stories from my life's journey.

To fully grasp the paradoxical nature of this relationship requires me to provide some context. The fact I exist within a society designed, built, managed and consumed by the majority of human beings who are unlike me, means this has always had consequences for those of us who are subjected to what I call, 'disablement' and 'disablism'. I will define these concepts in due course.

My lens on the world changed when I was in my early twenties and I realised how I was being seen and treated related to the nature of capitalism. Fifty years ago, this worldview was held by a small minority of people, and I was privileged to have the opportunity to discuss it with Paul and Judy Hunt who both assisted in creating the Disabled People's Movement.[1] The discussion led me to come to terms with disability.

Coming to terms with disability

Last year, *Pluto Press* published my book, *Disability Praxis*, in which I critiqued disability politics among other things.² Central to disability politics is the need to acknowledge that 'what disability is' is contested on many fronts. One ramification of the differences that exist in how disability is defined is that people who are impaired often see themselves differently from one another, as well as being treated differently by other people who are referred to as either 'able-bodied' or 'normal'. Part of the argument I will further here is that, despite views to the contrary, the *nature* of disabled people's oppression is unlike other forms of oppressive practice.

Disabled scholar activist, Mike Oliver, developed two theoretical models which he used to explore the dominant approach to viewing disability within capitalist societies and a counter-hegemonic approach developed by people with significant impairments who are oppressively subjected to dominant views and practices. He explored the dominant approach towards disability via what he termed, 'the individual tragedy model of disability'.³

The basic argument centres upon the view that the needs of Capital and the nature of capitalist social relations created disablement which has led to the conditions whereby people with significant impairments are either excluded from or marginalised within mainstream social activities. The need for an exploitable workforce led to an appraisal of 'the body' to determine which individuals were, and those who were not, fit for work. People with significant impairments were caught up in these medicalisation processes. In pre-capitalist society, divisions did exist but predominantly to control and discipline the 'idle able-bodied poor' as opposed to groups collectively viewed as 'impotents'.

The 'individual tragedy model of disability' explores how individual bodies that are pathologized as 'impaired' become defined by dominant ideologies and practice as being 'disabled'. The premise in this approach towards disability is that when our bodies/minds do not conform to the expected and accepted ways in which they are 'supposed' to function, this determines the nature and degree of how 'disabled' an individual person is. Crudely speaking then, 'the less one functions like a "normal person", the more "disabled" one can be judged to be.' Using this reductionist, judgmental, and oppressive evaluation of 'the body', society from the days of Bentham until the era of Neoliberalism, has legitimated seeing 'the disabled" (sic) as 'a tragic collection of individuals with personal deficits who, as a consequence, are lacking in social worth.'

Oliver's second model stemmed from people with physical impairments who, during the late 1960s and early 1970s, questioned why they were being unnecessarily segregated from mainstream society. The Union of the Physically Impaired Against Segregation (UPIAS) rejected viewing the impaired body as the root cause of people's social disadvantage, and relocated 'the problem of disability' as being to do with the nature of society and its failure to integrate physically impaired people into mainstream social activities. Hence they argued that the capitalist society transformed physically impaired people into 'disabled people' by imposing social restrictions.[4] From this social interpretation came Oliver's social model of disability and the political identity of 'disabled person/people' which denotes our social situation of being *disabled by society*.

While I broadly agree with UPIAS' social interpretation of disability, I believe there are two problematic areas within it. The first relates to how they view the process of disabled people's oppression. The second concerns how they view disabled people's social oppression in relation to what is spoken of as disablism in modern day disability politics.

UPIAS defined '... disability as the disadvantage or restriction of activity caused by a contemporary social organisation *which takes no or little account of people who have physical* impairments and thus excludes them from participation in the mainstream of social activities. Physical disability is therefore a particular form of social oppression'. [Emphasis added – BWF] [5]

While I believe the outcome of the impact of 'a contemporary social organisation' i.e., capitalist society, is captured here, what is absent is the ideological aspect of the creation of disablement. I would argue what is missing is the dialectic of disability; because it is *precisely how people with impairments are 'taken into account'*, in the sense of being subjected to negative evaluations and as consequence devalued, that ultimately leads to society taking little or no account of them. Without this dialectical understanding, the cause of social oppression can be simply viewed as either 'ignorance' or 'forgetfulness'.

I would argue UPIAS also unhelpfully collapsed together social oppression and discrimination. This is an all-too-common error within disability theory and politics. Paul Abberley remains one of only a few disabled scholars who questioned the nature of disabled people's oppression from a materialist perspective whereby there is a distinction made between oppression and discrimination.6 It is necessary to acknowledge the historical period in which both UPIAS and Abberley were writing and in the background was the new official definitions of impairment, disability, and handicap.7 These definitions were challenged by early disabled scholar activists.

Abberley argued that not all oppressions are identical and therefore it is necessary to explore how oppression operates, which means giving consideration to: 'its specificity, of form, content and location'. From this methodological stance he believed 'to analyse the oppression of disabled people in part involves pointing to the essential differences between their lives and those of other sections of society, including those who are, in other ways, oppressed'.8

While supporting this approach, I believe he offered a more rounded understanding of disabled people's oppression than UPIAS due to his assertion that to claim that disabled people are oppressed involves introducing several crucial areas for consideration:

- At an empirical level, it is to argue that on significant dimensions disabled people can be regarded as a group whose members are in an inferior position to other members of society because they are disabled people.
- It is also to argue that these disadvantages are dialectically related to an ideology or group of ideologies which justify and perpetuate this situation.
- Beyond this it is to make the claim that such disadvantages and their supporting ideologies are neither natural nor inevitable. Finally it involves the identification of some beneficiary of this state of affairs.9

My reading of these points is to acknowledge that oppression and discrimination are not one and the same but actually inform one another. The experienced of oppression stems from our inferior position to other members of society due to the combination of unequal and differential treatment as well as the devaluation of people with impairments as human beings. Dominant ideologies legitimate disabled people's social exclusion by maintaining a *causal link* between an individual's impairment and their social disadvantage. The radical social interpretation *breaks* this causal link. This does not mean ignoring the negative relational interactions that take place at the micro level of society where impairment reality is confronted by social restrictions that are often referred to as 'disabling barriers'. Disablism, I would contend, goes beyond discriminatory practices.

With many different definitions of 'disability' existing, and it being a contested area of debate, some disabled scholar activists like myself have shifted our focus in order to seek clarity. While maintaining that 'disability' denotes the social situation where people with impairments encounter imposed social restrictions; we prefer to speak of the creation of disablement as being the negative result of economic, political, social, and ideological influences on the structures, systems, values, culture and practice of given societies as encountered/experienced by disabled people. Whereas disablism is the acceptance and promotion of ideas and practice associated with dominant ideologies that present 'disability' as the absence of normality, a state of inferiority and the cause of perceived lack of social worth found within an individual, e.g., a burden on society, lacking in capacity.

In my theoretical and political work, I have not rejected the usage of 'disability' altogether. Maintaining the original UPIAS meaning of 'a social situation' created through imposed restrictions.

Being of this world, but not truly part of it – part one

You may be sat wondering how this heavy political stuff relates to me as a disabled supporter of sport and football in particular. I hope through talking about my engagement with sport it will become clearer as to what paradoxical relationships I encounter. In a generalised sense, the way society sees disability and disabled people has produced a paradoxical gaze between people with and without impairments which pictures each as 'alien' to the other; thus to the majority, I am viewed as well as being treated as 'Other'.[10] So, for the main part of my life, I have been made to feel 'of this world, but not truly part of it'. Disability politics have focused on changing social relations within society, but this has come at a high price in my opinion.

By focusing on changing what's going on 'out there', I believe the Disabled People's Movement neglected addressing at the same time the nature and impact of dominant ideologies on how disabled people often either internalise their oppression or lose their own sense of self. Disabled feminists were right to raise issues around living with impairments in a disablist society, but those issues are about personal experiences and encounters with disablism, not the collective structural social restrictions the social model was designed to explore. Clearly, there is a relationship between them, but nonetheless they relate to differing sites of struggle. Too little has been done to explore the impact our oppressive imposed identity has had on ourselves, individually, and on other disabled people, collectively.

Like most other oppressed sections of society, disabled people have had very few visible role models to rely on. Even today, the presentation of disabled people in the mass media or sport, remains framed either by the imposed identity or through a commodified cultural individualistic reversal of the dominant ways disabled people are viewed. Instead of the traditional 'Othering', disabled people – often spoken of as 'people with disabilities' (sic) – are encouraged to 'big up' their identity around the diversity contained within their own embodiment.[11]

Growing up 'invisible', without role models 'out there', I was never encouraged to be 'me'. The expectation was to be come as 'normal' as possible which, I would argue, distorted and held back any sense of self. While fully rejecting the ideological assertion that the nature and degree of a person's impairment is the direct cause of their social disadvantage, it is nonetheless a fact that our impairment reality is used against us. This point relates to Abberley's assertion about disabled people's inferiority; it is the nature of our impairment reality that leads to society singling us out for differential treatment. It is still the case that our 'self' is dressed in negativity with the expectation that we compare ourselves to others we have either never been like or are representative of our former selves. The failure of materialist disabled scholar activists to adequately explore the 'individual tragedy model' beyond how it underpins disabled people's experience of discrimination, opened the door to postmodernist critiques which reject to various degrees the foundations of the materialist grounding of the social interpretation of disability. Instead they focus on the cultural aspects of the dominant gaze.

I believe the emphasis upon prejudice and what is called, 'ableism', is misplaced. It is acknowledged that the binary able/disabled was socially constructed around the notion of 'ability'. Ability is a slippery concept as it can mean: 'possession of the means or skill to do something' or 'talent, skill, or proficiency in a particular area'. Words associated with ability include; capacity, capability, potential, power, and faculty. All these words and their meanings play key roles in making sense of the world and people within it. The hegemonic power of the use of meanings associated with 'ability' should not be underestimated. In all known societies there is evidence of people displaying their talents and skills, often in the form of competition. It is not possible however for me to discuss here how capitalism, misogyny, racism, and disablism have distorted or shaped how we view these human activities. I can nevertheless express concern about the notion of 'ableism' is currently employed.

Fiona Kumar Campbell in 2001 wrote:

> Ableism is a network of beliefs, processes and practices that produces a particular kind of self and body (the corporeal standard) that is projected as the perfect, species-typical and therefore essential and fully human. Disability then is cast as a diminished state of being human.[12]

However, Campbell goes on to state:

> Ableism systematically interacts with other power structures that stigmatize to produce race, gender, sex, and disability. Ableism shapes our world and produces disability; regimes of ableism have produced a depth of disability negation that reaches into the caverns of collective subjectivity to the extent that the notion of disability as

inherently negative is seen as a 'naturalized' reaction to an aberration.[13]

There are aspects of what constitutes 'ableism' which correspond to my understanding of 'disablism' however there are also a series of conflations at work in how 'ableism' is often employed. In the USA, it is not uncommon to see a rejection of 'ableism' stand alongside talking about 'people with disabilities' (sic).

Among my concerns about the articulation of 'ableism' is how it can be used in the practice of blaming and shaming. Crude interpretations have an internal logic which lead to the absurd conclusion that *all activities* which do not involve disabled people are by their very nature 'ableist'. This ignores how the social interpretation of disability speaks about 'unnecessary barriers', thereby acknowledging impairment reality. I believe a reactionary form of identity politics is fostering a dog-in-a-manger set of attitudes which is risking disabled people cutting off their noses to spite their face. Embracing diversity and 'difference' has consequences; it is not a one-way street.

There are those who argue 'ableism' and 'disablism' are one and the same, but I disagree. I view the notion of 'ableism' highly problematical and therefore retain the following definition of disablism:

WHITE LINES AND PARADOXICAL RELATIONSHIPS

Disablism is the acceptance and promotion of ideas and practice associated with dominant ideologies that present 'disability' as the absence of normality; a state of inferiority and the cause of perceived lack of social worth found within an individual, e.g. a burden on society, lacking in capacity to fulfil accepted and excepted tasks.

Disablism as a concept focuses on what causes and maintains social exclusion and marginalisation. Too often 'ableism' is reduced to being spoken of as 'the discrimination of and social prejudice against people with disabilities based on the belief that typical abilities are superior'.[14] Lewis defines ableism as:

A system that places value on people's bodies and minds based on societally constructed ideas of normality, intelligence, excellence, desirability, and productivity. These constructed ideas are deeply rooted in anti-Blackness, eugenics, misogyny, colonialism, imperialism and capitalism. This form of systemic oppression leads to people and society determining who is valuable and worthy based on a person's language, appearance, religion and/or their ability to satisfactorily [re]produce, excel and 'behave.' You do not have to be disabled to experience ableism'.[15]

This all-embracing view of 'a system' (sic) conflates so many issues into a single entity referred to as a form of systemic oppression; but who is actually subjected to this and why? I refer back to Abberley's final point about who benefits. Perhaps the final sentence from Lewis provides a clue as to why I believe this type of reductionism leads to a rabbit hole and Alice in Wonderland, along with a chocolate tea pot.

Me, myself and otherness

From an early age I was conscious of being different from the other children in my home town. I had been 'sent away to a special school' when I was five and a half. In my book, *More Than A Left Foot*, I outlined some aspects of growing up among other disabled children and my perceptions of the normal/abnormal divide.[16] I recall embarrassing my mother when I was eight by a retort I made to a stranger on the street who had approached her and said, 'Is he mental?'. Mother was too shocked to speak, however I said, 'I'm not, but you are!'

Being aware of being different and becoming conscious of the implications are not one and the same. As I moved towards my teenage years the 'difference' I felt and experienced became more to do with the question of social alienation. An example of my first awareness of social restrictions 'out there' coupled with the ignorance and biases intertwined with the social exclusion, occurred when I attended a local football match and witnessed Leighton Town playing badly. A man, three rows behind me, kept shouting out: 'What are you spastics playing at?' After becoming annoyed by this, I shouted: 'Oi mate, I wouldn't have that bloody lot in my team!' Not only did he stop shouting, but at half-time, he came over and apologised.

At the time, and perhaps for many years after, the profound and complex nature of my little quip failed to fully register with me. I had not only deflected back a disablist insult; in the same instance, I had asserted a positive identity for myself and those who were like me. In *More Than A Left Foot,* I wrote:

> Once I was involved in mainstream activity, I soon realised that I'd entered an unknown world inhabited by non-disabled people; a world I was in truth ill-equipped to deal with at the time. Here I want to introduce the notion of paradox. A paradox is said to be a statement that apparently contradicts itself and yet might be true. Having been in a segregated environment, my world had been quite 'normal', until I'd to consider what lay beyond it; the world of 'normal persons'. Once on the outside of the 'disabled' world, which had appeared 'normal', I was confronted by the world

of 'normal persons' and, subsequently, found myself to be 'disabled'.[17]

Recently, I came across a blog written by Brené Brown, where she conducted an interview with Psychotherapist and New York Times best-selling author Esther Perel. Ms Perel said:

> It's the ability to straddle contradictory beliefs, attitudes, feelings at the same time without having to think that it's an either/or, this or that.'[18]

In my opinion, this is what politically conscious disabled people do most of the time: we navigate paradoxical relationships. I believe Vic Finkelstein captured this when he gave this anecdote:

> 'You want to change the world?' The questioner asked with an expression of incredulity. I hesitated.
> Should I answer truthfully or back away as we so often did in public? We were attending a Central Television feedback meeting at a very early stage in the presentation of the Sunday morning LINK programmes. I had argued the case for a clear and open platform for the social interpretation of disability.

> We were not just pressing our case for the able-bodied world to accept us, to be more caring and make adjustments for our 'needs', but suggesting that the able-bodied world had to change – it was disabling us.
>
> 'Yes' I replied after a moment. 'We want to change the world' and with this I changed myself, my public identity, from a passive-dependent user of care services to an active citizen expressing my fundamental human right to have an impact on the world in which I live.[19]

Finkelstein's work is not always easy to 'interpret' because it is dangerous at times to take what he says at face value. He dialectically challenges dominant ideology through reverse psychology; he spoke of 'able-bodied people', and later to challenge the use of 'people with disabilities', he resorted to talking about 'people with capabilities'. Personally, I consider this style of provocation problematic within a landscape where nuance and irony are lost on the majority of disabled and nondisabled people.

What is key within the above quotation is the last paragraph – adhering to disability politics – politics which seeks to overthrow disability – changes one's public identity because being a disabled person becomes a political identity. I need to qualify this statement in two ways: firstly, I am talking about an identity which signifies *what* I am, rather than *who* I am. The identity refers to 'out there', not my personhood; this is why I disagree with viewing disability politics simply as a form of identity politics, as the objective of embracing the identity is different, as I will endeavour to explain. Secondly, what this also means is that those of us adjudged to be 'disabled', but also have a political understanding of this, end up with a 'dual identity' – 'disabled person' as defined by society, part of 'the disabled' (sic), and 'disabled person' as being subjected to social oppression.

Suggesting that the world has to change

It is possible to talk about changing the world in a variety of ways; betterment, reformism, and radical transformative agendas, for example. Within *Disability Praxis,* I raise questions around what it is that disabled people want, the dialectics involved in their emancipation struggle, and the paradoxical nature of our relations with capitalist society. The current paradox being that disabled people want to be 'included' in a world that is designed and managed to exclude or marginalise them. This necessitated a discussion around the differing meanings given to 'independent', integrated, and inclusive living. Mike Oliver and myself view 'inclusive practice' as a process not only to be 'struggled over' within existing sites of struggle, but also as part of disability praxis which is transformative of existing social relations. Inclusivity rejects viewing 'equality' as being sameness. The equality is established through the acknowledgement, acceptance, and furtherance of the diversity within lifestyles and experiences by giving them equal value.

Capitalism creates alienation through its social relationships however by producing disablement, it distorts these relationships even further for specific groups. How does this oppressive situation impact upon disabled people? Too many of my brothers and sisters remain locked away in residential institutions or trapped, isolated, in their own homes. Others, like myself, negotiate alien environments with their social restrictions.

How I managed to do my shopping without killing someone recently is hard to explain. Here is an account of one of my participatory engagement with society:

> My first error was placing my car fob too close to my purse. Having my purchases put through, I discover my card doesn't work and I don't have enough cash to pay for it all. That's when the fun started. Living all my life with a speech impairment, I have developed an in-depth analysis of how handicapping normality can be for nondisabled people. A number of factors come

together to create disablism. My speech is unusual, sometimes it is difficult to understand without the employment of good listening skills, but too often that isn't the problem. Having set their gaze on my body, their brains panic and go into shut down think mode and switch over to emergency freak stereotyping reliance. By relying on stereotyping, it is irrelevant how clearly I speak, because their normality has deafened them and therefore they stop listening. Without the ability to communicate and think, they resort to the only abilities they can rely on. They seize control of the situation; seeking quick solutions to the abnormal problem they are confronted with.

The situation becomes a battle of wills. I manage to negotiate to pay for the goods I can, promising – times three – to return with cash for the remaining items. Off to the bank I go, and when there, I explain the problem. The cashier however insists I put the card in the machine, then the Einstein tells me the card isn't working – normality is obviously catching! Finally, I get the cash and go back to the supermarket. Perhaps by now you can guess what's coming?

No one listens or knows what I'm talking about. I explain: 'There's shopping behind there I've come to pay for'. The response I received was:

'Why would it be behind here? Can't see any; unless you mean these?'

It would appear I am dealing with Ms Einstein this time. She tells me to feed the machine, and I state that I am unable to physically do that. This exchange is repeated a number of times. While I am taking a note out and sorting the right change, suddenly without warning, Ms Einstein grabbed a higher domination out of my purse and slots it into the machine before leaving me to scoop up the change. If this isn't disablism, what is it? I was socially restricted by their crippling normality.

People's common-sense ideas about normality relies on assumptions and stereotypes; whether or not they think they are superior is neither here nor there because what determines these forms of interpersonal interactions is the deep-rooted contours around what is or is not considered 'normal'. I would suggest these contours influence disablism. In the supermarket and the bank, what I encountered is called disablism. Disabled people attempt to live 'ordinary lives' but we are prevented from doing so by a disabling world full of paradoxical relationships. We are encouraged to participate, but denied the ability to do so, expected to conform to 'normal social relations', but penalised when we fail to do so. We are made invisible as a result of society's norms and values being offended by our visible nonconformity; unless we are portrayed as 'brave' and 'struggling to overcome disability – although not too much as it is embarrassing to see! People with invisible impairments or chronic illnesses face a double bind: they are socially made invisible, yet at the same time because the disabling gaze cannot fall on them, they are judged to be fakers or have their needs ignored. Disabled people's 'unequal and differential treatment' takes an array of specific forms.

Being of this world, but not truly part of it – part two

Paradoxical relationships also occur when disabled people seek to mingle with nondisabled people on their own turf when we take on the role of spectator. Within a world primarily designed by and for social actors without impairments, then most activities will cater for their needs and will reflect their desires and interests to a great extent. Within this generalisation is the need to recognise class and cultural diversity. Outside inclusively designed or specifically created activities for disabled people, the culture we observe is undertaken by nondisabled people.

I have no desire to be a separatist, to cut myself off from the rest of humanity simply because they are not impaired and live in the same disabling world, but are not directly impacted by it. As socialists, disabled or not, there is a need to consider our values and engagement in social activities outside of work and how we both perceive and evaluate them.

Let me place disablism within the context of paradoxical relations with an example.

My first live football match was in 1962 where I watched Watford beat Swindon two nil. Football, and sport in general, has been an aspect of my life however it has never been a straight forward part of my being or the culture I embrace. This is probably true, of course, for nearly every aspect of my life, but the nature of sport itself produces tensions and contradictions unlike any other relationship I have. Football is a physical sport where men and women use their bodies beyond any capacity that I could ever have. I do not envy or resent them for being able to do what they do. I accept my impairment reality; my oppression exists and is maintained because society refuses to.

I love the poetry of football, all manner of things are played out on the pitch, with physical and mental capacity often being tested to the full. Football combines collective and individual endeavour. I am aware that some people question sport which relies on competition, arguing that having 'winners' and 'losers' can be damaging. Firstly, I believe rivalry exists in all kinds of social relationships and these need to be managed. Challenging ourselves and others is part of learning and development. This does not negate activity or sport that is not competitive. As an aside, I abhor 'the Special Olympics' because they are patronising and oppressive, yet on the other hand, they provide learning disabled people an opportunity to engage in sport.

I am a football supporter, not a 'commodified fan'. White lines are boundaries, they mark when the ball is out of play; the game is paused. So when the players cross the white line the realities of the world and my impairment, the paradoxical relationships I have to negotiate, are put on hold unless my access needs are denied. That, of course, is another story.

NOTES

1. Hunt J., *No Limits,* TBR Imprint, 2019.
2. Williams-Findlay B., Disability Praxis: The Body as a Site of Struggle, Pluto Press, 2023.
3. Oliver M., *The Politics of Disablement,* London, Macmillan,1990.
4. Union of the Physically Impaired Against Segregation, *Disability Challenge* 1, 1981, p.7.
5. Finkelstein, V., 'Phase 2: Discovering the Person in "Disability" and "Rehabilitation"', *Magic Carpet*, Vol XXVII (1), 1975, pp.31-38, p.33.
6. Abberley, P., 'The Concept of Oppression and the Development of a Social Theory of Disability' in *Disability Studies: Past Present and Future,* edited by Len Barton and Mike Oliver, pp.160-178, p.162-3, Leeds: The Disability Press, 1997.
7. Harris, A. I., Smith, C., Cox, E. & Buckle, J. R., *Handicapped and impaired in Great Britain*, London: Great Britain: Office of Population Censuses and Surveys, H.M.S.O, 1971.
8. Abberley, P., 'The Concept of Oppression', 1997, p.162
9. Ibid.
10. Sullivan, K., 'Otherness and the power of exclusion', 2015, https://www.sipri.org/commentary/blog/2015/otherness-and-power-exclusion. See also Chapter Seven in Williams-Findlay, R., *More Than a Left Foot*, London: Resistance Books, 2020.
11. Ema Loja, Maria Emília Costa, Bill Hughes & Isabel Menezes, 'Disability, embodiment and ableism: stories of resistance', *Disability & Society*, 28:2, 2013, pp.190-203. Hughes, Bill, and Kevin Paterson, 'The Social Model of

Disability and the Disappearing Body: Towards a Sociology of Impairment', *Disability & Society* 12 (3), 1997, pp.325–334. Dickel, S., 'Disability and Embodiment' in: *Embodying Difference*. Palgrave Macmillan Cham, 2022.

12. Campbell, Fiona Kumari, 'Inciting Legal Fictions: Disability's date with Ontology and the Ableist Body of the Law', *Griffith Law Review*, 10(1), 2001, pp.42 – 62, p.44.
13. Campbell, F. K., 2001, p.61
14. , 'First there was racism and sexism, now there's ableism', BBC, 2014, https://www.bbc.co.uk/news/blogs-ouch-27840472, Withers, A. J., 'Disablism or Ableism?', 2013, https://stillmyrevolution.org/2013/01/01/disablism-or-ableism/
15. Lewis, T. A., 'Working Definition of Ableism', 2021, https://www.talilalewis.com/blog/january-2021-working-definition-of-ableism.
16. Williams-Findlay, B., *More Than a Left Foot*, London, Resistance Books, 2020.
17. Williams-Findlay, B., 2020, p.135
18. Brown, B., 'Partnerships, Patterns, and Paradoxical Relationships', 2021, https://brenebrown.com/podcast/partnerships-patterns-and-paradoxical-relationships/
19. Vic Finkelstein, 'We Want to Remodel the World', Editorial prepared for the 10th anniversary of the founding of the London Disability Arts Forum (LDAF) and published in the DAIL magazine, 1996, https://disability-studies.leeds.ac.uk/wp-content/uploads/sites/40/library/finkelstein-Remodel-the-world.

3

Developing an eco-social approach towards self-determined living

The aim of this article is to look in more detail at the issues and methods of working behind the idea of developing an eco-social approach towards supported living as proposed by the vision adopted by the campaign group, Act 4 Inclusion, at its 2021 AGM.[1] The article seeks to explain key definitions and positions which could bring together ecological and social models. What is important to remember is that the A4I vision is organic, therefore, it remains in a state of development and that the views here are primarily my interpretation of their vision.

Definitions employed

The meaning of disability
Talking about 'disability' or 'disablement' is always difficult because different meanings are attached to each word. In dominant thinking, they can refer to an

individual's impairment or condition, the impairment's impact on bodily function, or its consequences for participation.

Globally, many do not make a distinction between 'impairment reality' [personal restrictions and/or characteristics] and encountered social restrictions] disabling barriers; hence, they talk of 'people with disabilities' and 'disability pride.'[2]

In Britain, the social approach does not see 'disability' as a personal attribute or characteristic, but rather as an oppressive outcome of the negative interactions caused by society not addressing the unnecessary social restrictions imposed on people with significant impairment. As a result, language usage between American and British disabled activists often differs. Hence many US activists see 'disability rights' as being 'the rights belonging to people with disabilities.'

I believe the radical British social approach views 'disability rights' as being 'rights *standing in opposition to* disability.' This is an important, but rarely understood, political distinction.

This difference in meaning or understanding has implications for how Disability Justice might come to be viewed in Britain.

'Disability Justice' originates in America: Disability Justice centres intersectionality and the ways diverse systems of oppression amplify and reinforce one another. It is a term that is often used interchangeably with terms such as 'disability rights' and 'disability inclusion.' Yet it's important to recognise that 'disability justice' refers to a very specific framework of thinking about disability; it is an American approach; so how could its ten principles be understood and articulated in Britain?

Disability inclusion is a broad term to describe approaches to advance access and inclusion for disabled people. A disability justice approach centres the priorities and approaches of those most historically excluded groups, such as women, people of colour, immigrants, and people who identify as LGBTQ+.[3]

What is 'climate justice'?
It begins with the idea that the adverse impacts of a warming climate, are not felt equitably among people.

Key points:
1. Climate justice recognizes key groups are differently affected by climate change.
2. Climate impacts can exacerbate inequitable social conditions.

Momentum is building for climate justice solutions.

Framing the debate
While international research is making a more concerted effort to actively include some populations in

communication and strategies, the disability community has been consistently omitted.

The wide-ranging exclusion is concerning, as climate change is expected to affect disabled people in three ways:

1. most likely to have limited access to knowledge, resources, and services to effectively respond to environmental change;
2. more vulnerable to extreme climate events, ecosystem services loss, or infectious diseases;
3. more likely to have difficulties during required evacuations or migrations.[4]

In a United Nations Survey a high proportion of disabled people were found to either be injured or even die during natural disasters. This was due to a lack of consultation with disabled people and governments that lacked necessary measures to support and protect them. Only 20% of respondents to the survey said that they could evacuate immediately and 6% said that they could not evacuate at all.[5]

The needs of disabled people are often not considered; such as accessible evacuation centres, transport for the individual, any essential equipment they need to manage their impairment and health conditions, information in formats that they can read and understand, for example, communication tools for deaf and visually impaired people.

Lateef H. McLeod, an American activist and writer, wrote an article in which he explores commonalities between social ecology and disability justice in their respective visions for liberation. He explains:

> Focusing on the shared components of anti-capitalist critique, mutual aid or interdependence, and ecological sustainability, I will illustrate how these two movements can align to build a more just, egalitarian, and ecologically sustainable world. I argue that social ecology and disability justice share a variety of values and goals that make them natural partners in struggles for collective liberation.[6]

Tensions between climate justice and disability justice do exist:

> The emphasis on cycling, and its framing in opposition to driving, and the dominant narrative of self-sufficiency, are both exclusionary and discriminatory. With links to individual health and independence, this could reinforce pervading neoliberal attitudes that may perpetuate the oppression faced by disabled people.

Unless we can get disabled people working and integrating in the core fabric of the environmental sector, we're not gonna be able to make these connections and the world is not gonna see how environmental justice and inclusion is linked so closely to disability equality and inclusion.[7]

Lateef argued:

For social ecologists to be in solidarity with the disability community they must consider disability justice principles in any transition from capitalism. Social ecologists and other parts of the left also need to include the disability community more in their organizational strategies and making changes, to ensure this goal is achieved. At a basic level, this requires paying more attention to access needs people may need in your group. This reflects the ninth disability justice principle of collective access.[8]

We can see numerous connections between environmental problems, the creation of impairment and disablement: lack of clean water, pesticide poisoning, air pollution, oil spills, mercury contamination, silicosis, worker safety in extractive industries, and climate-induced migration, to name but a few.

DEVELOPING AN ECO-SOCIAL APPROACH

If environmental justice seeks the fair treatment of all people with respect to environmental decisions and policy, then disabled people must be part of the discussion, and yet they are regularly excluded from decision-making and face discrimination. Unless this is addressed, it could mean climate solutions and adaptation plans may be designed without their needs in mind, and they may not have equal access to green jobs, and opportunities of a just transition. For climate movements, it means they are missing valuable perspectives, talent, and experience that could broaden and enrich their agendas and increase their power to create systemic change.

The principle of collective access is not simply about ensuring physical access into buildings or transportation, nor it is just about developing 'inclusive' practice either. Collective access has to be created by recognizing the inequalities that exist in power relationships, the fact that diverse groups of people are impacted upon by normative values and oppressive practices differentially. Inclusive practice requires addressing intersectional issues, managing conflicts of need and interest, as well as drawing on the creative imagination and experience of different groups of people. Vic Finkelstein in 1980 said:

> The requirements are for changes to society, material changes to the environment, changes in

environmental control systems, changes in social roles, and changes in attitudes by people in the community as a whole. The focus is decisively shifted on to the source of the problem -the society in which disability is created.[9]

Social model of disability revisited

The radical social model switched the focus away from looking at an individual's loss of functioning in body activity as the root cause of their participation disadvantage and instead centred upon how the social organisation of society creates restrictions and disabling barriers. The objective is to identify how policy, practice, design and socially built environments, *disable* differing groups of people with impairments and seek ways to address the barriers and social restrictions.[10] The 'unequal and differential treatment' experienced by disabled people results in discrimination, disempowerment and is subsequently viewed as a form of social oppression.

How should environmental, structural and attitudinal barriers that impinge upon the lives of disabled people be addressed to ensure disabled people gain the maximum possible self-determination in daily living activities, to achieve mobility, to undertake productive work, and to live where and how they choose to live their lives? Disabled people identified barriers to 'independent living' and what is required to address them. Whilst the 12 Pillars of Independent Living set out addressing the barriers, there is no acknowledgement of the fact individuals and groups interact within differing social and natural environments and systems.[11] This is where ecological theory can assist the social model of disability.

The road ahead

Developing an eco-social approach towards disability will only have any real significance if it embedded across social movements such as Climate Justice and the interests of marginalised sections of society are actively taken onboard. Disability Justice and an eco-social approach towards disability will have commonalities and differences. However, the success of both requires strong and organised voices to defend the interests of disabled people, children, women and older people because the impact of climate change and the deepening of the ecological crisis could be catastrophic for these groups, especially in the poorer nations of the world where abject poverty is the norm rather than the exception for those at the foot of the social hierarchy. In the current circumstances we urgently need, as Len Barton wrote in 2001 speaking about sociology, but it equally applies to the development of an eco-social approach towards disability:

> a political analysis which is inspired by a desire for transformative change and that constitutes hope at the centre of struggles ... At both the individual and collective level a crucial task is to develop a theory of political action which also involves the generation of tactics or strategies for its implementation. This is a difficult but essential agenda.[12]

Developing a radical eco-social approach towards a new system capable of producing and sustaining community-based services needs to be part of this process.

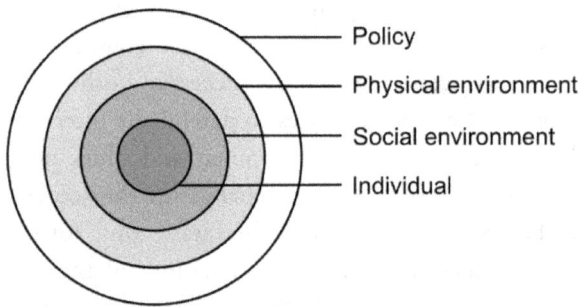

Using the ecological and social models together would enable us to consider the impacts and adaptions that correspond to climate, ecosystems and society issues. There is some common ground between what Act 4 Inclusion is advocating and ideas found within green social work, however, there are possible differences as well. Within the social model, the meaning given to 'social' contains the assertion that the organisation of society needs to change as it maintains 'normative values' based upon class interests.

To what extent existing eco-social approaches consider disabled people from the perspective we favour is debatable. Shogren et al., for example, outline social-ecological models of disability, but are any of them compliant with the radical social model?[13]

The ways in which social models have hitherto been employed, pay little attention to the various systems or levels within society where social restrictions are encountered. For example, at the micro level, we are seeking to address the personal lifestyles of individuals in terms of where they live, what support they need, their relationships with other people, etc. At the medium level, the encountered restrictions may occur within neighbourhoods, communities, groups of people or accessing work, leisure activities.

All community activities, such as education, leisure, employment and day care, are part of the exosystem which is the third level. 'Exos' in Greek means outside or external. The exosystem thus comprises of institutions and influences that are external to the individual, and yet exert a decisive influence on their psycho-social development.

At the macro level, we are considering the impact of existing health and social care systems, laws, market forces, state perspectives, etc. There are interactions and impacts across all levels.

The defining feature of an ecological model is that it takes into account the physical environment and its relationship to people at individual, interpersonal, organisational and within communities.

Act for Inclusion (A4I) share and promote the following as a baseline for developing a new system. This would mean embracing:

- Recognition of the dignity and worth of all human beings, respect and appreciation for diversity and the assumption, identification, and recognition of strengths and potential of all human beings;
- Recognition of the interconnectedness among the systems;
- The importance of [promoting] advocacy and changes in socio-structural, political, and economic conditions that disempower, marginalize, and exclude people; and, ;
- The need to focus on capacity-building and empowerment of individuals, families, groups,

organisations and communities through a human-centred developmental approach.[14]

A4I believes it is possible to encourage a human-centred developmental approach by adapting existing ways of working, including what is known as 'person-centred planning'.[15]

Disabled people in the UK developed the social model of disability, arguing for a shift in the balance of power between people and the services on which they rely. Person centred planning is based in the social model of disability because it places the emphasis on transforming the options available to the person, rather than on changing the person or slotting them into existing services. Specifically person-centred planning was based diversely on principles of community integration/inclusion. Not to be confused with neoliberal 'Personalisation'.[16]

Person-centred planning involves asking:

- *Who are the important people in a person's life?* These are the people the person wants to be involved in developing their person-centred plan and who can help them make things happen. These are the committed people in the person's life: family, friends and others who know and care about them. They are the person's circle of support.

- *What are the person's desires, things they enjoy doing?* Finding out what the person's current lifestyle is like and what they might want to change, develop or take up. For example, are there specific kinds of employment, educational courses, career paths, day or social activities they may wish to pursue?
- *What is important to the person now and in the future (their dreams)?* This helps the person think about what is important to them in their life. Some things will already be present and will need to continue, whilst other things will need to be planned for. Learning about what is important to the person can also help others to understand their preferences. Similarly, blue sky thinking (asking what a person's dreams are) can provide ideas about what to pursue in the future.
- *What kinds of support will the person need to achieve the future they want?* People will need to identify key areas in which support is needed, and to talk about how they can get that support. This should adopt a holistic approach.

A4I state that they want to see the development of a new national service framed by a community based eco-social system which needs to work for all disabled people, of all ages, with all types of impairment, and for everyone in society. A community based eco-social

DEVELOPING AN ECO-SOCIAL APPROACH

system would take an intersectional approach towards policy making, considering the differential impact of universal and targeted policies across the diversity of disabled people.[17]

Recognising and acknowledging the different levels or systems within society enables us to consider the interaction, impact and consequences of what takes place within them. In terms of the individual and particular groups, it assists us to identify and address social restrictions that exist within their immediate or distant social environments. This includes the impact of both social and physical environments on their existing or future lifestyles.

Through coproduction, policies at national and local levels would be developed with the aim of producing community-based services that fostered inclusivity and sustainability.

Making physical environments, transport, information technologies, etc. more accessible to disabled people whilst at the same time benefiting families, communities, and society as a whole. Ensuring that the national service delivered locally develops sustainable strategies to protect natural and built environments and resources.

Many names have been given to disabled people's right to self-determination. Independent, Integrated, or Inclusive Living, can be developed through a community based eco-social system ensuring civil and human rights. A community based eco-social system of delivering services would take a holistic approach using coproduction.[18] By acknowledging interdependency and inequality of power relations, we can foster new social arrangements which allows disabled people to have greater control over their own lives. This includes the opportunity to make real choices and decisions regarding where to live, with whom to live and how to live.

The new eco-social system would develop policies and practices aimed at facilitating the removal of barriers and coproducing inclusive practices in a holistic interactive approach to diverse lifestyles:

- Social support services within mainstream communities
- Universal public services - e.g., NHS
- Eco-long-life housing
- Transportation
- A transformative social security system
- Access to Justice
- Education and training
- Accessing paid employment and other opportunities
- Sustainable communities and accessible natural environments

Conclusion

I believe Act 4 Inclusion are under no illusion; they acknowledge their vison does not offer quick-fix solutions, and neither do they believe the majority of social actors involved in Social Care provision will readily embrace the eco-social approach. Nonetheless, A4I are committed to their vision because it offers the opportunity to articulate a transformative agenda that has the potential to make real differences in people's lives.

Notes

1. At its Annual General Meeting on 21 May 2021, Reclaim Social Care adopted a new name, vision and strategy.
2. See 'My Disability Lexicon and Disability Politics and Culture: Seeking A Bridge Over Troubled Waters'.
3. See Chapter 9, 'A Radical Eco-social Approach Towards Sustainable Community-based Services', in B. Williams-Findlay, *Disability Praxis*, London: Pluto Press, 2023
4. Aleksandra Kosanic, Jan Petzold, Berta Martın-Lopez and Mialy Razanajatovo, 'An inclusive future: disabled populations in the context of climate and environmental change', https://www.researchgate.net/publication/358884324_An_inclusive_future_disabled_populations_in_the_context_of_climate_and_environmental_change.
5. 'UN survey focuses on how persons with disabilities cope during disasters', https://news.un.org/en/story/2013/07/445732; 'The results show limited progress in disability inclusion over the past 10 years, with no significant differences across the regions', quoted from the '2023 Global Survey Report on Persons with Disabilities and Disasters', https://www.undrr.org/report/2023-gobal-survey-report-on-persons-with-disabilities-and-disasters,
6. Lateef H. and McLeod, 'Social Ecology and Disability Justice: Making A New Society', https://harbinger-journal.com/issue-1/social-ecology-and-disability-justice/.
7. Fenney D., 'Ableism and disablism in the UK environmental movement', The Free Library, 2017, The

White Horse Press, 28 December 2024, https://www.jstor.org/stable/26407805
8. McLeod.
9. Finkelstein V., 'Attitudes and Disabled People: Issues for Discussion. World Rehabilitation Fund, New York, 1980, p.22, https://disability-studies.leeds.ac.uk/wp-content/uploads/sites/40/library/finkelstein-attitudes.pdf
10. Mike Oliver, *Understanding Disability: From Theory to Practice*, London: Macmillan Press, 1996, p.30-42.
11. See Chapter 4 'The Third Cornerstone: Self-Determination, De-Institutionalisation and Promotion of Self-Directed Living' in *Disability Praxis*. 'Twelve pillars of independent living', https://enil.eu/independent-living/
12. Barton, L., *Disability, struggle and the politics of hope. In Disability, politics and the struggle for change*, ed. L. Barton, pp. 1–10, London, 2001.
13. Karrie A. Shogren, Michael L. Wehmeyer, Jonathan Martinis and Peter Blanck, 'Social-Ecological Models of Disability', in *Supported Decision Making: Theory, Research, and Practice to Enhance Self-Determination and Quality of Life*, Cambridge Disability Law and Policies Policy Series, Cambridge University Press, 2018, pp. 29–45.
14. Boetto H. and Bowles W., 'Eco-social transition: Exploring the wisdom of our elders', in Matthies A. Närhi K. (eds), *Ecosocial Transition of Societies: Contribution of Social Work and Social Policy*, Abingdon, Surrey, Routledge, 2017, pp. 190–205.
15. 'What is a person-centred approach?', *National Disability Practitioners*, 2016, https://www.ndp.org.au/images/factsheets/346/2016-10-person-centred-approach.pdf.
16. Bob Williams-Findlay, 'Personalisation and Self-determination: The Same Difference?', *Critical and Radical*

Social Work, Vol. 3, No.1, Bristol: Policy Press, 2015, 67–87.
17. Sins Invalid, '10 Principles of Disability Justice', 2015, www.sinsinvalid. org/blog/10-principles-of-disability-justice. See also Chapter 9 in *Disability Praxis*.
18. Boyle D. and Harris M., The challenge of co-production: how equal partnerships between professionals and the public are crucial to improving public services, London: Nesta, 2009.

4

My disability lexicon

Introduction

I have put together key concepts and definitions based upon the social approach towards disability as applied to my writing. The definitions of disability politics, culture, and art all operate through a juxtaposition of opposing forces, for example, disability politics are viewed as 'politics standing in opposition to disabling social restrictions'.

Key concepts

Disability: the imposition of social restrictions on top of impairment reality created from the structures, systems, values, culture and practice of given societies which creates an oppressive situation - exclusion and/or marginalisation. Disability therefore is an encountered oppressive social situation.

Disablement: is the negative result of economic, political, social, and ideological influences on the structures, systems, values, culture and practice of given societies as experienced by disabled people.

Disablism: the acceptance and promotion of ideas and practice associated with dominant ideologies that present 'disability' as the absence of normality, a state of inferiority and the cause of perceived lack of social worth found within an individual, e.g., a burden on society, lacking in capacity to fulfil accepted and excepted tasks.

Social oppression: the historical development of 'unequal and differential treatment' of people with impairments which has led to their exclusion from or marginalisation within mainstream societal activities.

Disability discrimination: 1. action or inaction by institutions or individuals which produce or lead to social restrictions 2. Creating or engaging in unequal and differential treatment because of someone's actual or perceived impairment.

Disability hate crime: the deliberate act of engaging in unequal and differential treatment with wilful intent because of someone's actual or perceived impairment. Within UK law impairment and disability are conflated (see Disability definition in Equality Act 2010).

MY DISABILITY LEXICON

The following definitions work through the dialectical relationship between disability (social restriction) and emancipatory engagement.

Disability rights: sets of demands by disabled people to further self-determination and in opposition to their social oppression. Not simply the legal protection of their civil and human rights.

Disability culture: the cultures developed by disabled people in their struggle for emancipation from disability. It is therefore a political counter-culture which rejects 'normality' and societal evaluation of living lives with impairments.

Disability pride: the expression of defiance (often as celebration of being who and what we are) against unequal and differential treatment and a demand for social justice, equality and acceptance.

Disability art: production of material that recounts or challenges disabled people's lived experience of unequal and differential treatment as part of the emancipation struggle

About the publisher

RESISTANCE BOOKS is a radical publisher of internationalist, ecosocialist, and feminist books. Resistance Books publishes books in collaboration with the International Institute for Research and Education (https://iire.org/), Anti-Capitalist Resistance (https://anticapitalistresistance.org/) and the Fourth International (https://fourth.international). For further information, including a full list of titles available and how to order them, go to the Resistance Books website.

info@resistancebooks.org
www.resistancebooks.org

 Click on the QR code for Resistance Books

About ACR

AntiCapitalist Resistance is an organisation of revolutionary socialists. We believe red-green revolution is necessary to meet the compound crisis of humanity and the planet.

We are internationalists, ecosocialists, and anti-capitalist revolutionaries. We oppose imperialism, nationalism, and militarism, and all forms of discrimination, oppression, and bigotry. We support the self-organisation of women, Black people, disabled people, and LGBTQI+ people. We support all oppressed people fighting imperialism and forms of apartheid, and struggling for self-determination, including the people of Palestine.

We favour mass resistance to neoliberal capitalism. We work inside existing mass organisations, but we believe grassroots struggle to be the core of effective resistance, and that the emancipation of the working class and the oppressed will be the act of the working class and the oppressed ourselves.

We reject forms of left organisation that focus exclusively on electoralism and social-democratic reforms. We also oppose top-down 'democratic centralist' models. We favour a pluralist organisation that can learn from struggles at home and across the world.

We aim to build a united organisation, rooted in the struggles of the working class and the oppressed, and committed to debate, initiative, and self-activity. We are for social transformation, based on mass participatory democracy.

info@anticapitalistresistance.org
www.anticapitalistresistance.org

 Click on the QR code for Anticapitalist Resistance.

Coming to terms with disability is part of the Resistance Books Pocket Books series, a publishing initiative of ACR. Recent titles include:
- *Labour's Extreme Neoliberalism*, Jamie Gough
- *Resisting Trumpism*, Daniel Tanuro, Paris Wilder, Gilbert Achcar, Simon Hannah & Echo Fortune
- *Manifesto for an EcoSocialist Revolution,* Fourth International
- *Making Sense of Russia's Invasion of Ukraine,* Paul Le Blanc
- *Capitalist China and Socialist Revolution*, Simon Hannah

www.ingramcontent.com/pod-product-compliance
Lightning Source LLC
Chambersburg PA
CBHW070804040426
42333CB00061B/2460